MY ANGER IS OUT
OF CONTROL

Jim Newheiser

Consulting Editor: Dr. Paul Tautges

My Anger Is Out of Control

© Jim Newheiser 2014

ISBN
Paper: 978-1-63342-072-4
ePub: 978-1-63342-073-1
Kindle: 978-1-63342-074-8

Shepherd Press
P.O. Box 24
Wapwallopen, PA 18660

www.shepherdpress.com

All Scripture quotations are from the New American Standard Bible (NASB). Copyright © 1995 by The Lockman Foundation.

First printed by Day One Publications

Designed by **documen**

CONTENTS

Introduction   5

1 Understanding Anger   9

2 How Can Angry People Be Helped?   25

3 Overcoming Anger by God's Grace   29

4 Practical Ways You Can Overcome Anger   39

   Conclusion   51

   Personal Application Projects   55

   Where Can I Get More Help?   59

   Notes   61

Introduction

Anger is widespread. A star tennis player forfeits a match because she screams threatening profanities at a line judge. A motorist in traffic expresses road rage by pulling a gun. Every day we hear about crimes of abuse, assault and even murder in our communities. We may hear our neighbors screaming at each other and wonder if we should intervene. Anger is also a major issue among professing Christians. Jay Adams writes, "Sinful anger probably is involved in ninety percent of all counseling problems."[1] In my experience I am not sure that anger is not involved in the other ten percent.

Angelo's wife Cheryl betrayed his trust by getting into a compromising situation with another man. She has repeatedly and tearfully confessed her sin to him and sought his forgiveness, but each time she tries, Angelo calls her a whore and threatens to divorce her. "It is over!" he tells her.

Grace gets upset when her husband Rolly seems to ignore her when she tries to address the problems in their marriage. About once a week she flies into a rage, often cursing and sometimes hitting him. Recently she threw a large vase down the stairs. Rolly is concerned for his own safety and that of his children. The neighbors have called the police more than once. Though Grace is usually remorseful the next day, Rolly is considering taking the children and moving out of the home. Grace feels helpless against her rage.

Patty was thrilled to have the opportunity to work as a personal assistant for John, a well-known Christian author and speaker. In recent months, however, Patty has wondered whether she should have taken this job. John's ministry has been under a great deal of financial pressure and John's time is over-committed. He then takes out his stress on Patty, frequently chewing her out for minor mistakes. Patty is shocked that this "great man" treats her worse than her secular bosses did. She doesn't know where to turn and is not sure if anyone would believe her if she told them what John was really like.

Jane has been married to Peter for over twenty-five years. Peter is a domineering husband who micro-manages Jane's life and that of their children (until they reached adulthood and escaped). Peter is constantly grumpy – yelling at the traffic, shouting at the politicians on TV and complaining about the church leaders (who never realized Peter's great potential and therefore kept him on the sidelines). Jane has outwardly played the role of the quiet submissive wife, rarely arguing or retaliating, but inwardly she is full of bitterness. Finally, she realizes that she will never please this man and decides that she can't stand living this way, so while Peter is at work she packs up and leaves. Peter returns home to an empty house, not even having a clue of why his wife is gone.

Bob is a successful Christian businessman who is glad to employ many believers in his company. He uses a substantial portion of his profits to support various Christian ministries. Bob, however, in his drive for success, often publicly berates workers who don't meet his expectations. His Christian employees are shocked by his behavior, but no one has the nerve to confront him. They also notice that Bob seems to change churches every few years.

Why Do We Act this Way?

Angelo would say that Cheryl deserves to be told off after what she did to him. Grace, on the other hand, would admit that she is deeply ashamed after an eruption of rage. She wishes she could stop. Some have told her that her anger may be a disease. Perhaps the right pill would stop her from such outbursts. John would say that Patty's on-the-job failures put the future of the ministry at risk. Peter might say that he just has a strong personality, while Jane would say that now that the kids are grown she doesn't have to put up with being verbally abused by a selfish, angry man. Bob would say that he is a highly driven leader which is what has led to the success of his company that benefits customers, employees, and Christian organizations. Strong words get results. Results benefit everyone.

While different people express anger in different ways, anger is a challenge for every Christian. Some feel powerless in the face of anger. Others try to justify themselves. The question we must address is how can a sinfully angry person become a person of grace? The answer is that the Gospel of Jesus Christ transforms angry people into gracious people.

1

Understanding Anger

Anger is a concept which can be hard to put into words. You know when you are angry and you can often tell when someone else is angry, but it is hard to give a precise definition. Charles Spielberger, PhD, a psychologist who specializes in the study of anger says, "anger is an emotional state that varies in intensity from mild irritation to intense fury and rage."[2] Biblical Counselor Robert Jones states, "Anger is our whole-personed active response of negative moral judgment against perceived evil."[3] Or, more simply, anger is an emotion which arises out of a judgment.

Common Characteristics of Anger

ALL ANGER SEEMS RIGHTEOUS.

Because we are in God's image we have a sense of justice. We become angry because we believe that an injustice has taken place. Sadly, because we are fallen and sinful, our view of justice is distorted. The injustice which most offends us is when our personal rights have been violated. This inward sense of injustice stirs our hearts to desire to make things right or even, which involves executing appropriate judgment or revenge (Romans 12:17-21).

ANGER HAS A PHYSICAL COMPONENT.

Our body and our soul are connected. What affects one usually affects the other. The American Psychological Association recognizes this reality. "Like other emotions it is accompanied by physiological and biological changes; when you get angry, your heart rate and blood pressure go up, as do the levels of your energy hormones adrenaline and noradrenaline."[4] We see examples in Scripture of how heart anger affects people physically. When the Lord rejected Cain's offering, "Cain became very angry and his countenance fell" (Genesis 4:5). The physical effect of Moses' anger is described, "as soon as Moses came near the camp, he saw the calf and the dancing and Moses' anger burned" (Exodus 32:19). Biblical words for anger reflect the physical component of anger – burning, trembling, and flaring nostrils. Anger can be linked to sleepless nights, loss of appetite, and digestive problems.

ANGER IS ACTIVE.

Angry people often act on their anger by words or deeds, some of which can be very dramatic and impactful. For example, Moses "threw the tablets from his hands and shattered them at the foot of the mountain. He took the calf which they had made and burned it with fire and ground it to powder and scattered it over the surface of the water and made the sons of Israel drink it" (Exodus 32:19-20).

ANGER IS DECEPTIVE.

Hebrews 3:13 warns us against the deceitfulness of sin. Sinfully angry people typically try to justify their anger by claiming that it was righteous. An abuser will say that his victim deserved what she got. A person who has been guilty of a hateful profanity-laden tirade will claim, "I didn't really mean it." It may be that he now wishes that he had never said what he did, but at the time he meant every word of it. Merely claiming that he didn't mean it will not undo all of the damage he has done. Some try to deny their anger by calling it something else as they shout, "I'm not angry, I'm just frustrated!" It is also common for angry people to say that their anger is caused by something outside of themselves. Often they will blame other people. A pastor claimed that if a certain church elder were to be removed from the board, his anger problem would be solved. An angry woman will say, "If my husband would just change I wouldn't get angry." We shall see that Scripture teaches that we can never honestly say, "You made me mad!" because our anger comes from within our hearts and is not caused by anything outside of us (Mark 7:14-23). Circumstances and people squeeze us and show what is inside of us. On the other hand, most people can be fairly pleasant if they always get their own way (as if they are like God!). Other people try to excuse their anger by blaming genetics or their upbringing. We will deal with these excuses in the next section.

ANGER IS DANGEROUS.

The comic book character Dr. Bruce Banner appears to be a mild-mannered gentleman until he is stressed or angry, which causes him to become the Incredible Hulk, a monster who destroys property and hurts people. Many people who struggle with anger are similar to Dr. Banner. They can sometimes seem quite normal and calm, but when provoked they become enraged and do great harm, especially to those who love them. While many people want to minimize the seriousness of their anger, especially if they have not become physically violent, Jesus teaches that sinful anger is murderous by nature. "You have heard that the ancients were told, 'You shall not commit murder', and that 'Whoever commits murder shall be liable to the court.' But I say to you that everyone who is angry with his brother shall be guilty before the court; and whoever says to his brother, 'You good-for-nothing,' shall be guilty before the supreme court; and whoever says, 'You fool,' shall be guilty enough to go into the fiery hell" (Matthew 5:21-22). John writes, "everyone who hates his brother is a murderer" (1 John 3:15). Anger in the heart can lead to actual acts of physical assault or murder, as was the case when Cain murdered Abel (Genesis 4:5-8) and when the Jews stoned Stephen (Acts 7:54-60). James warns that sinful heart desires often lead to deadly acts of sin (James 1:14-15). Those who give in to anger are at risk of losing control. "Like a city that is broken into and without walls is a man who has no control over his spirit" (Proverbs 25:28). Psychologists also recognize this reality, "when it (anger) gets out of control and turns destructive it can lead to problems at work, in your personal relationships and in the overall quality of your life. And it can make you feel as though you're at the mercy of an unpredictable and powerful emotion."[5] In counseling I have been grieved to witness spouses saying hateful things to one another including, "I hate you. I wish I had never married you. You repulse me. I wish you would divorce me. I could kill you." Such hateful words can never be taken back and create wounds which are very difficult to heal. "With his mouth the godless man destroys his neighbor" (Proverbs 11:9). "There is one who speaks rashly like the thrusts of a sword" (Proverbs 12:18).

Paul warns that anger gives the devil an opportunity to wreak his murderous havoc in your relationships. "Do not let the sun go down on your anger and do not give the devil an opportunity" (Ephesians 4:26-27). I once asked a husband whose besetting sin was verbally blowing up at his wife and child what he would do if a criminal was at the door of his house trying to break in to do harm to his family. He replied that he would fight with all of his might to keep his family safe. I then said that his anger is an equally serious threat to the well-being of his family and that when he gives in to his rage, he is inviting the devil into his home. He needs to resist his anger as vigorously as he would fight an intruder.

ANGER, LIKE THE LOVE OF MONEY, ALSO LEADS TO MANY OTHER SINS.

"An angry man stirs up strife, and a hot tempered man abounds in transgressions" (Proverbs 29:22). Sinful anger can lead to the violation of every one of God's commandments. In anger, people have stolen property, committed immorality, lied, murderously destroyed relationships, dishonored parents, and have put themselves in the place of God as lord and judge. Anger is often related to other harmful emotions including bitterness, depression, anxiety and fear.

ANGER ALSO IS CONTAGIOUS.

"Do not associate with a man given to anger or go with a hot tempered man or you will learn his ways and find a snare for yourself" (Proverbs 22:24-25). "A harsh word stirs up anger" (Proverbs 15:1). Angry people often tempt others to sinful anger. Entire families and churches can become consumed by this sin. God's grace is the only cure.

ANGER IS NOT NECESSARILY SINFUL.

God Himself gets angry and justly expresses His holy anger. "The anger of the LORD burned against Moses" (Exodus 4:14)... "He will speak to them in His anger and terrify them in His fury... do homage to the Son, that He not become angry and you perish in the way" (Psalm 2:4-5,12). "The anger of the LORD burned against that land to bring upon it every curse which is written in this book" (Deuteronomy 29:27). Jesus expressed righteous anger when he drove the money changers out of the temple (John 2:12-17). On another occasion Jesus, "looking around at them with anger, grieved at their hardness of heart" (Mark 3:5).

When is anger righteous?

Righteous anger is rare among sinners like us. Robert D. Jones has identified three characteristics of righteous anger.[6]

1. RIGHTEOUS ANGER REACTS AGAINST ACTUAL SIN.

Those against whom Jesus was angry were guilty of sinfully using God's holy temple for unholy purposes. Spurgeon writes, We do well when we are angry with sin because of the wrong which it commits against our good and gracious God.[7] If no sin has taken place, we have no right to be angry. For example, if we were to be angry at someone who is late because they got caught in unpredictable traffic then our anger would be unrighteous because they didn't commit any sin.

2. RIGHTEOUS ANGER FOCUSES UPON GOD AND HIS KINGDOM, RIGHTS AND CONCERNS, NOT ON ME AND MY KINGDOM, RIGHTS AND CONCERNS.

Because we are sinners we are inclined to make ourselves the center of the universe and to judge those who don't submit to our will. The intensity of our anger is usually not in proportion to the sin against God's kingdom, but rather according to the damage we perceive to our own personal interests. In contrast, Jesus' anger against the temple merchants was motivated by a zeal for His Father's house. In other words, is your anger because God didn't get what He wants, or because you didn't get what you want?

3. RIGHTEOUS ANGER IS RIGHTEOUSLY EXPRESSED.

Even when a real sin has taken place and one thinks he is concerned for God's kingdom interests, anger is not righteous if it is expressed sinfully. For example, one may have righteous anger against an abortion clinic in the community because the unlawful taking of human life is a sin against God Who has made humankind in His image. But if this anger is expressed through hateful speech and violence against people and property, the anger is not righteous and does not serve the interests of God's kingdom. My experience in counseling is that many counselees can identify actual sins committed against them and they may claim that their anger is due to their zeal for God's kingdom, but it is rare that such anger is expressed in a God-honoring way. Instead, many resort to destructive speech, bitterness and rage, often feeling fully justified because they have been sinned against.

What causes out-of-control anger?

Secular psychologists tend to blame either nature (genetic predisposition) or nurture (social environment). The American Psychological Association states, "Some people get angry more easily and more intensely than the average person does...(demonstrating) a low tolerance for frustration, (and are) particularly infuriated if the situation seems somehow unjust... One cause may be genetic or physiological; there is evidence that some children are born irritable, touchy and easily angered... Research has shown that family background plays a role. Typically, people who are easily angered come from families that are disruptive, chaotic, and not skilled at emotional communications."[8] Some claim that they struggle with anger or rage because of hormonal issues or as the side effect of certain medications.

SCRIPTURE DEALS WITH MOST ANGER AS A SIN ISSUE.

Put them all aside: anger, wrath, malice, slander and abusive speech from your mouth (Colossians 3:8). As we have already seen, Jesus teaches that wrongful anger is murderous (Matthew 5:21-22). While it is possible that some of us may be more tempted to anger because of genetic makeup or social environment, these factors can never be used as an excuse for sinful behavior.[9] Each of us is sinful by nature (Romans 3:23 Isaiah 53:6) and we live in a fallen and broken environment. Every person is tempted by sin in various ways. Some who are not as tempted by anger may be more drawn to substance abuse, sexual immorality, or worry/fear. The believer can be confident that God will never allow him to be tempted beyond what he is able to bear (1 Corinthians 10:13), and as a new creature in Christ (2 Corinthians 5:17) he has been set free from slavery to sin (Romans 6:3-7).

THE BIBLE TEACHES THAT ALL SIN, INCLUDING ANGER, BEGINS IN THE HEART.

Jesus said, "That which proceeds out of the man, that is what defiles the man. For from within, out of the heart of men, proceed the evil thoughts, fornications, thefts, murders, adulteries, deeds of coveting and wickedness, as well as deceit, sensuality, envy, slander, pride and foolishness. All these evil things proceed from within and defile the man" (Mark 7:20-23). In the context Jesus is explaining that what goes into a man (unclean food) is not what defiles him, but that which is already in his heart makes him unclean (Mark 7:14-19). In the same way, our external circumstances, including what people do against us, do not make us sinfully angry. All they do is expose the sin which is already in our hearts. That means our hearts must be changed if we are to overcome anger.

WE BECOME ANGRY BECAUSE WE WANT SOMETHING (TOO MUCH).

James raises the question, "What is the source of quarrels and conflicts among you? Is not the source your pleasures that wage war in your members? You lust and do not have; so you commit murder. You are envious and cannot obtain; so you fight and quarrel" (James 4:1-2a). Secular psychologists recognize the same dynamic. "The underlying message of highly angry people is "things oughta go my way!" Angry people tend to feel that they are morally right, that any blocking or changing of their plans is an unbearable indignity and that they should not have to suffer this way".[10] When you feel yourself becoming angry, you should ask yourself, "What is it that I want so much?" The angry person believes that he has a right to what he desires. His anger is active judgment upon whoever keeps him from getting what he thinks he deserves. It is important to understand that it may be that the desire of the person prone to anger is legitimate – i.e. a mother wants her children to be obedient and respectful; or a husband wants his wife to be supportive and affectionate; or a wife wants her husband to pay full attention and understand her; or a boss wants his workers to perform with excellence.

Each of the people described in the introduction became angry because others were failing to meet what they believed to be their legitimate desires. But a legitimate desire becomes a sinfully idolatrous desire when it becomes a controlling desire. We know a desire is idolatrous when we are willing to sin in order to get what we want, or we become sinfully angry if we don't get what we want. The answer to idolatry (false worship) is true worship. James continues, "You do not have because you do not ask. You ask and do not receive because you ask with wrong motives, so that you may spend it on your pleasures" (James 4:2b-3). Rather than seeking ultimate satisfaction from other people who will often let us down because they are sinners, we need to turn to God to meet our needs. "Ho! Every one who thirsts, come to the waters; and you who have no money come, buy and eat. Come buy wine and milk without money and without cost. Why do your spend money for what is not bread, and your wages for what does not satisfy? Listen carefully to Me and eat what is good, and delight yourself in abundance" (Isaiah 55:1-2). The person who is hoping that other people will meet his needs will never find true peace and satisfaction (Jeremiah 17:5-8) and thus will be tempted to anger when others fail him. The person who seeks satisfaction in Christ will have a joy and a peace which can't be shaken by the sins and failures of others. When angry, ask yourself, "What am I seeking and treasuring more than I seek and treasure Christ?"

Angry people believe that they possess certain rights, including the right to express their anger when their rights are violated.

The angry person is self-centered and proud. He tends to minimize his own sin and magnify the sins of others. He is obsessed with what he believes to be his rights. For example, many husbands focus upon the duty of their wives to submit, but seem to spend little time meditating on what it means to sacrificially love one's wife as Christ has loved the church (Ephesians 5:22-30).

ANGRY PEOPLE LEARN THAT THEIR ANGER OFTEN GETS RESULTS.

They discover that they can manipulate others with their anger, thereby seeming to get what they want. The mother might say, My kids won't obey unless I scream at them. The wife discovers that her husband doesn't do household chores unless she bitterly nags him (but see Proverbs 21:9). The husband discovers that if he acts grumpy and bitter, his wife may try to pacify him with physical affection. There are many bullies in families, neighborhoods, workplaces and even churches who use anger to control others and to get their way.

In the end angry people experience loss, including the loss of their idols. Even though sinful anger seems justified in the moment and despite the fact that sometimes anger produces desired results in the short term, angry people wind up suffering the consequences of their sin (Galatians 6:7-8). The angry person often experiences overwhelming stress, lack of peace, financial loss, and broken relationships as a result of his sin. What real joy is there in getting your way, when others are just placating you and then seek to avoid you whenever they can? Angry people often find themselves alone. The very desires and demands for which they were willing to fight remain unmet.

But is there hope? Can the angry person change? Can we change? Yes, with the Lord's grace all sinful behaviors can be overcome. We will learn how in Chapter 3. But before we get there, let's briefly consider a few secular methods that fall short of lasting change.

2

How Can Angry People Be Helped?

Secular psychology promotes "anger management." "The goal of anger management is to reduce both your emotional feelings and the physiological arousal that anger causes."[11]

Psychologists encourage their clients to manage anger through expressing, suppressing and calming. "Expressing your angry feelings in an assertive — not aggressive — manner is the healthiest way to express anger... This (suppressing) happens when you hold in your anger, stop thinking about it and focus on something positive. The aim is to inhibit or suppress your anger and convert it into more constructive behavior... This (calming) means not just controlling your outward behavior, but also controlling your internal responses, taking steps to lower your heart rate, calm yourself down, and let the feelings subside."[12] Some take anger management classes which teach strategies to try to keep anger at bay, including relaxation, cognitive restructuring, communication techniques, humor and changing one's environment. "Simple relaxation tools such as deep breathing and relaxing imagery can help calm down angry feelings... When you get angry and call someone a name... stop and picture what that word would literally look like. If you think of a coworker as a dirtbag, picture a large bag full of dirt sitting at your colleague's desk, talking on the phone, going to meetings... Picture yourself as a god or goddess, a supreme ruler who owns the streets and stores and office space, striding alone and having your way in all situations while others defer to you... If your child's chaotic room makes you furious every time you walk by it, shut the door."[13]

These methodologies do not adequately address the heart of anger. Secular psychology fails to understand the nature of mankind. We are not merely physical creatures shaped by genetics and environment, but we are spiritual beings created in God's image. We are fallen and sinful by nature, which is at the root of most of our anger. While secular counselors may teach some basic techniques for behavior modification, secular psychology is powerless to address the sin/heart issues and to effect true inward spiritual change (Romans 8:7-8).

Sadly, many professing Christians have been influenced by secular psychology as they try to deal with anger. I have heard some Christians, including at least one pastor, speak about having to "vent" their anger by getting it all out. Scripture says, "A fool always loses his temper, but a wise man holds it back" (Proverbs 29:11). Others internalize their anger which results in bitterness and resentment which often erupts at a later time. Many also try to excuse their anger by blaming their nature/genetics (which would essentially be blaming God Who made them James 1:13); others blame their environment/other people (which also would be blaming God who controls all things (Ephesians 1:11 Romans 8:28). I have been grieved to see Christian pastors send their members who struggle with anger and other spiritual issues to secular counselors whose techniques only deal with the symptoms of anger, rather than pointing them to the answers contained in the all-sufficient Scriptures (2 Timothy 3:16-17).

The foundation of biblical anger management is the gospel of Jesus Christ. All of us are sinners who have failed to keep God's perfect law (Romans 3:23). Our just God has every right to be angry with us and to punish us for our sins (Romans 6:23). Jesus Christ has come into the world and has taken our guilt upon Himself and died in our place (2 Corinthians 5:21). All who repent of their sins and believe upon Him are not only freely forgiven, but are given the rich gift of perfectly righteous standing before God (Philippians 3:9; 2 Corinthians 8:9). Have you confessed your sinfulness to God and believed upon Him? Only those who have experienced His grace can show such grace and forgiveness to others. "All of us like sheep have gone astray, each of has turned to his own way; but the LORD has caused the iniquity of us all to fall on Him" (Isaiah 53:6).

Now let's turn to the Scriptures to examine God's methods for life-change that lasts.

3

Overcoming Anger by God's Grace

Mild-mannered Dr. Bruce Banner, when he becomes angry, is transformed into the hideous Incredible Hulk. When Dr. Banner starts to get stressed, his friends and colleagues try, often unsuccessfully, to calm him down before he becomes The Hulk and goes into an uncontrollable rage. Many people, like Dr. Banner, need help dealing with their anger. In reality, it is the truth of the gospel which doesn't merely restrain anger, but actually puts out the fires of rage and replaces them with the cool waters of grace.

The key to overcoming anger is what you say to your own heart (Proverbs 4:23), especially in seasons when your anger might be provoked. An angry person has given into untrue wicked lies in his own heart. He tells himself how righteous he is while he judges the other party to be worthy of wrath. He tells himself that his rage is justified and that he can't help himself. He thinks that the only way that he can control his anger is if the people and circumstances in his life change in accord with his desires. He may say, "When I am angry I don't think, I just react." Scripture teaches that it is very dangerous to just let our minds wander as they will, on autopilot (Proverbs 14:12). We are responsible (and in Christ able) to direct our thoughts according to truth (Philippians 4:8-9).

"Don't make me count to ten!"

James 1:19 reminds us to be slow to anger. Some counselors recommend that an angry person count slowly to ten before saying or doing anything. While angry people often cool down a bit over time, the heart issues are not addressed by mere delay. When the next provocation takes place anger often picks up where it left off last time.

Five crucial biblical truths an angry person must consider.

Instead of merely counting to ten, or to a thousand, an angry person needs to stop and fill his mind with biblical truth so that he can overcome anger in his heart and become a person of grace. When anger is building these truths do not automatically come to mind. Actually the angry person is suppressing these truths so that he can continue to feed, justify, and express his rage. He must learn in the crucial moments of temptation to set his mind on things above because he is united with Christ (Colossians 3:1-3). I often give a counselee a practical assignment of writing the following five truths on a notecard to be carried at all times so that as soon as temptation comes these truths and the related Scriptures can be reviewed. These biblical truths redirect our hearts from devilish anger to Christian grace.

I want something too much – which is idolatry (James 4:1-4).

We become angry when our desires are not met. What must you have in order to be happy? Must you be respected and appreciated? Comfortable? Successful? Must you have a stress-free life? We must give our desires to God as we seek our ultimate satisfaction in Him (Isaiah 55:1-2; Psalm 34:8). When we are willing to sin in order to obtain what we desire or to be sinfully angry because our desires have not been met, we have made these desires into idols. See the personal application projects at the end of this booklet for an assignment to help you identify your idolatrous desires.

I am not God/Judge
(Genesis 50:19; Romans 12:17-21)

When others wrong us, we sense that the balance

of justice is out of kilter and we want to make it right again. The angry person thinks to himself, "You wronged me, so you deserve to be punished." The angry person can punish the guilty party through hateful speech, acts of violence, slander, theft, or more subtly through being cold, quiet and withdrawn. All of these expressions of anger are sinfully judgmental. James reminds us that contrary to what our sinful hearts may think, "The anger of man does not achieve the righteousness of God" (James 1:20). Our vengeful acts do not bring justice, but rather they compound sin. "Never pay back evil for evil to anyone... Do not be overcome by evil, but overcome evil with good" (Romans 12:17, 21). Even worse, our sinful expressions of anger usurp God's office as judge.

> "Never take your own revenge, beloved,
> but leave room for the wrath of God, for
> it is written, 'Vengeance is mine, I will
> repay, says the Lord.'"
>
> (Romans 12:19)

After their father Jacob died, Joseph's brothers were fearful that Joseph would take revenge upon them for all the evil they had done to Joseph years earlier when they, out of jealousy, left him in a pit to die and then sold him as a slave (Genesis 37:18-28; 50:15). These guilty men begged Joseph to forgive them, and even claimed that Father Jacob had given instructions that Joseph show them grace[14] (Genesis 50:16-18). Joseph weeps and says, "Do not be afraid, for am I in God's place?" (Genesis 50:17b, 19). In other words, Joseph says that even though he has the right and power to punish them, he refuses to play God by judging his wayward brothers. Also, when others wrong us, we can be comforted that God will bring justice to those who do evil, even when human systems of justice fail. As we trust Him, we don't need to take our own revenge or play God.

God has been very gracious to me–in Christ (Ephesians 4:31-32; Matthew 18:21-35).

When we realize that each of us is "foremost (chief) among sinners" (1 Tim. 1:15) and that we have been forgiven an overwhelming debt, our hearts will be moved to show grace to those who have wronged us. Jesus tells the parable of the unmerciful servant who had been forgiven a great debt, which would be billions of dollars in today's money (Matthew 18:23-27)[15], but he then sought out his fellow slave who owed him what would have been thousands of dollars in today's money[16], but a tiny fraction of what the first slave had been forgiven. The forgiven slave "seized him and began to choke him, saying, 'pay back what you owe'" and then had his fellow slave cast into prison, ignoring his pleas for mercy (Matthew 18:28-30). The result was that their master heard what had happened. "Then summoning him, his lord said to him, 'You wicked slave, I forgave you all that debt because you pleaded with me. Should you not also have had mercy on your fellow slave, in the same way I had mercy on you?' And his lord, moved with anger handed him over to the torturers until he should repay all that was owed him" (Matthew 18:31-34). Jesus then warns, "My heavenly Father will also do the same to you, if each of you does not forgive his brother from your heart" (Matthew 18:35). Here we see that the gospel is the key to overcoming anger. When I dwell in my heart upon the hundred denarii debt my brother owes me, I, like the wicked slave, become angry and want revenge. When I remember and meditate upon the mercy God has shown me at such a great price (2 Corinthians 9:8) by which Jesus paid my infinite debt on the cross, I cannot stay angry at my brother or sister. He who has forgiven me calls upon me, for His sake, to be gracious to others as He has been gracious to me. Secular anger management techniques involve suppressing or redirecting the fires of anger. The gospel actually puts out the fires of anger and replaces them with the living water of grace.

I also believe that it is significant that the debt of the second servant is not merely a tiny amount. Most of us would be quite disturbed over losing thousands of dollars. This illustrates that during the course of life in a fallen world, our fellow sinners may hurt us in significant ways. A spouse may be unfaithful. A child may become wayward and cause great heartache and expense. A friend may betray a trust. A business partner may cheat you out of a substantial amount of money. None of these compares, however, to the debt God has forgiven us in Christ. The gospel has enabled believers to overcome anger and bitterness and to offer forgiveness and grace. "Let all bitterness and wrath and anger and clamor and slander be put away from you, along with all malice. Be kind to one another, tender-hearted, forgiving each other, just as God in Christ also has forgiven you" (Ephesians 4:31-32).

God is in control and is doing good for us.
(Genesis 50:20 Romans 8:28)

After Joseph refused to judge his brothers he added, "As for you, you meant evil against me, but God meant it for good in order to bring about this present result, to preserve many people alive." Joseph was able to act graciously towards his brothers because he had sound theology. He believed in a God who is sovereign over all things, even the evil done to us by others. Further, Joseph believed that God was working through these events for good for His beloved people. As we have seen, angry people want to be in control and become upset when things don't go their way. The angry person must submit to God, trusting that He is exercising His sovereignty for His glorious purposes and for our good. "The Lord has established His throne in the heavens and His sovereignty rules over all" (Psalm 103:19). When people fail you and circumstances go against you, God is at work. He uses trials to produce maturity and Christlikeness in His people (James 1:2-4; 1 Peter 1:6-7). We can also trust that He Who is sovereign over all things and Who knows us perfectly will not allow us to be tempted beyond what we can bear (1 Corinthians 10:13). He will provide a way for you to respond to each trial without sinful anger, but with grace and hope.

Remember who you are – a new creature in Christ (Romans 6:11; 2 Corinthians 5:17).

Angry people often feel stuck in their patterns

of rage and helpless to change. While it is true that unbelievers are enslaved to sin, those who are united with Christ by faith have been set free from sin's bondage. We have died to sin once and for all and are now united with Christ in newness of life (Romans 6:4-7). We are now new creatures in Christ (2 Corinthians 5:17), no longer controlled by the flesh, but filled by the Holy Spirit Who is producing His wonderful fruit in our lives (Galatians 5:13-23). The person who blows up in anger is going back to his old pre-Christian life. When he tells himself that he can't control his anger, he is lying to himself and denying his new status in Christ. How we think of ourselves is determinative of how we act. Paul's first command in his epistle to the Romans is "Even so consider ourselves to be dead to sin, but alive to God in Christ Jesus" (Romans 6:11). The person who gets sinfully angry has forgotten his new gospel identity in Christ.[17]

When we are tempted to respond to people or circumstances with sinful anger, it is the renewal of our minds with these biblical truths that will empower us to walk in grace and humility.

4

Practical Ways You Can Overcome Anger

The Christian has great resources by which he can not only put off anger, but put on grace.

Five Ways God's Grace Empowers Change

By God's empowering grace you can glorify God and be a blessing to others, including those whom you've hurt in the past through sinful anger.

1. God's grace enables you to exercise patience and self-control.
"A man's discretion makes him slow to anger. It is a glory to overlook a transgression" (Proverbs 19:11). "He who is slow to anger has great understanding" (Proverbs 14:29). "He who is slow to anger is greater than the mighty. He who rules his spirit than he who captures a city" (Proverbs 16:32). Many claim that they can't control their temper, when the reality is that they sinfully choose not to

do so. Jay Adams tells a story of the young mother who is having a terrible afternoon. The dinner has burned, the children are acting up. She finally erupts with volcanic anger, but then when the phone rings, suddenly the mother immediately calms down and answers, "Hello Mrs. Green. It is so good to hear from you."[18] I was once counseling a Marine sergeant who was guilty of frequently venting his anger on his wife and children, claiming that he could not help himself. I asked him if he ever hits them and he proudly declared, "I would never do that." This man has the ability to control himself, but he chooses to do so only under certain circumstances. I could have also asked if he ever speaks to his superior officers the way he speaks to his wife and I am sure that he would have said no. For the believer, self-control and patience are the fruit of the Holy Spirit's work in his life. As he walks in light of the gospel, patience and self-control will come forth. Paul also warns that if we fail to walk by the Spirit, we may fall into enmities, strife, outbursts of anger, disputes, dissentions and factions (Galatians 5:16,19-20). By God's grace we can be like God Himself who is slow to anger (Exodus 34:6).

2. God's grace enables you to speak with gentleness and grace.

"A gentle answer turns away wrath, but harsh words stir up anger" (Proverbs 15:1). Gentleness and humility can be disarming when other people are angry at you. A wife whose husband is grumpy and impatient can respond with compassion and gentleness, rather than retaliating. As formerly angry people have their hearts transformed, their words become gracious and build others up. "Let no unwholesome word proceed from your mouth, but only such a word as is good for edification according to the need of the moment, so that it will give grace to those who hear" (Ephesians 4:29). Those who used to tear others down with their words can learn to speak in a way that builds others up.

3. God's grace enables you to humbly receive correction even when is done hurtfully.

"Do not reprove a scoffer or he will hate you, reprove a wise man and he will love you" (Proverbs 9:8). A pastor who had been harshly criticized by a disgruntled member replied, "I am sure that you are right that I fall short of what I should be in so many ways. I am amazed at God's grace and that of His people that I am allowed the privilege to serve in the church. I want to learn how to better serve Christ and His people." When Shimei harshly cursed David, the King refrained from angry revenge as he trusted that God had a good purpose in Shimei's hurtful words (2 Samuel 16:5-13).

4. God's grace enables you to show love to those who hurt you.

After Joseph's brothers, who had done such evil against him came to him, he not only granted them forgiveness but he also showed them great love and kindness. "So therefore, do not be afraid; I will provide for you and for your little ones. So he comforted them and spoke kindly to them" (Genesis 50:21). Likewise, Paul encourages us not only to leave vengeance to God, but also to do good to our enemies by caring for their physical needs (Romans 12:20-21). This of course reflects God's love to us in that while we were His enemies He still loved us and did good for us (Matthew 5:43-48; Romans 5:8). He not only forgives us of our guilt, but also blesses us with every spiritual blessing (Ephesians 1:3). Showing love instead of anger to those who hurt us fulfills the exhortation, "therefore be imitators of God, as beloved children; and walk in love, just as Christ also loved you and gave himself up for us, an offering and sacrifice to God as a fragrant aroma" (Ephesians 5:1-2).

5. God's grace enables you to pursue the restoration of those who hurt you.

"Brethren, if anyone is caught in any trespass, you who are spiritual, restore such a one in a spirit of gentleness; each one looking to yourself so that you will not be tempted. Bear one another's burdens, and thereby fulfill the law of Christ" (Galatians 6:1-2). Jay Adams points out that anger may usefully energize us to address problems that we would otherwise ignore.[19] When we recognize that our brother's transgression is primarily against God and not us (Psalm 51:4), then we can focus on restoring our wayward brother to right relationship with God, rather than judging our brother by venting our sinful self-centered anger. In order to be truly helpful we must be spiritual, that is characterized by the fruit of the Holy Spirit (Galatians 5:22-23) which will lead to healing, as opposed to being fleshly which will only lead to more angry conflict. We also are able, in the Spirit, to correct gently, remembering that we too are sinners who need grace from God and others. We also can be motivated to gentleness by recalling that it is hard to receive correction. No one enjoys other people poking in his or her eye, even if the intention is to take out a dangerous speck. Of course it is also important that we be sure that any logs in our own eyes have been removed before we attempt to do surgery on our brother or sister (Matthew 7:1-5).

Four more practical principles

1. Don't be quarrelsome.

"The beginning of strife is like letting out water, so abandon the quarrel before it breaks out... for lack of wood the fire goes out and where there is no whisperer, contention quiets down. Like charcoal to hot embers and wood to fire, so is a contentious man to kindle strife" (Proverbs 17:14, 26:20-21). Often when an argument breaks out the most important issue is not the topic of the quarrel but the way you are treating each other. The effects of angry words and looks can be felt long after the topic of discussion has been forgotten.

2. Deal with anger and conflict quickly.

Jesus teaches that resolving conflict is so important that one should even interrupt worship in order to make things right with a brother who has something against you (Matthew 5:23-24).

Paul warns, "Be angry and do not sin; do not let the sun go down on your anger" (Ephesians 4:26). Sometimes it may seem convenient to leave conflict unresolved. After time passes both parties cool down, but the heart issues remain. A seedling of bitterness can, over time, become a sequoia of hate and resentment. Marriages and friendships have been ruined because the sun set too many times on sinful anger.

3. Prepare for temptation.

"The plans of the diligent lead surely to advantage, but everyone who is hasty comes surely to poverty" (Proverbs 21:5). In the same way that a person who struggles with drunkenness needs a plan for the time when friends invite him to a drinking party, or when his heart feels drawn to his old way of life, a person who has frequently given in to sinful anger needs a plan for how she will deal with tempting situations. One possible plan is to read and recall the five key things to tell yourself (along with the Scriptures) when one feels anger rising up in his heart.

4. Continually seek God's help through prayer.

We know our own weakness in the face of sin. We

cannot bear any fruit apart from abiding in Christ
(John 15:5). What a blessing it is to have a Savior
Who sympathizes with our weakness, was tempted
in all ways as we are tempted, and Who intercedes
for us! "Let us draw near with confidence to the
throne of grace, so that we may receive mercy and
find grace to help in time of need" (Hebrews 4:16).
Pray before temptation comes so you will be ready.
Pray for help in the time of temptation so you may
respond with grace and not judgment. Ask others
to pray with and for you.

Three Common Questions

1. **What does it mean to be angry and yet not
    sin (Ephesians 4:26)?**
Is Paul encouraging or making allowance for
a certain kind of anger which isn't particularly
wrong? I don't believe so. Paul seems to be making
the same point as James does in 1:19, "Be slow to
anger." Because you are in God's image you will
react against perceived injustice. Because you are
fallen and sinful, you will often immediately feel
the heat of anger when someone provokes you.[20]
At that point you have a choice. Rather than
allowing that anger to take up residence in your
heart, deal with it quickly and righteously. Then

the devil doesn't have opportunity to wreak havoc in your life and in the lives of others.

2. Is it ever permissible to be angry with God?

People sometimes talk about being angry with God. Some even (wrongfully) regard it as therapeutic to express such anger. Many don't fully grasp the implications that their anger at circumstances is ultimately anger against God. The soldier who is furious because of the atrocities he saw on the battlefield; the mother who is angry because her husband will not change and her children remain unconverted; the man who is bitter because his wife died; and the girl who doesn't like her physical appearance may all be angry with God because He did not do what they thought He should do. The prophet Jonah was very angry with God, both because God showed mercy to Israel's enemies the Ninevites and because the plant which gave him shade died (Jonah 4:1-9). God responded with remarkable restraint (Jonah 4:10-11). It is never permissible, however, to be angry with God. Such anger presumes that God has somehow been unjust. Furthermore, the person who is angry with God places himself above God as His judge, which is both wrong and dangerous (Romans 11:33-36).

We are free to respectfully express our questions to God (Habakkuk 1:1-4; 12-17; 2:1) and to lament our sorrows (Psalm 13:1-2; 42:9; 43:2). Ultimately we have to submit ourselves to Him who is both sovereign and good, even when we don't fully understand His ways (Deuteronomy 29:29).

3. What if you are angry with yourself?

Sally had an abortion when she was in her late teens. Now, twenty years later, she is childless. She spends every Mother's Day weeping over her guilt and sorrow. George wasted a great job opportunity several years ago and since then has struggled both in his career and with his finances. He sometimes feels like he hates himself for being such a failure in life. How can a person who is angry with himself be helped? Often we are angry with ourselves because of pride. We are upset because our life goals won't be fulfilled. We may think, "I am better than that, or I didn't live up to my standards." We may also be afraid of what others may think of us (Proverbs 29:25) because of our sins and failures.

The answer to anger with self is to remember that the only verdict which matters is that of God Who has declared you righteous for Christ's sake. "And may be found in Him, not having a righteousness of my own derived from the law, but that which is through faith in Christ, the righteousness which comes from God on the basis of faith" (Philippians 3:9). Just as God has not appointed you judge of others, He has not called you to be your own judge. Some who are angry at themselves punish themselves by verbally running themselves down in front of others or even by cutting themselves physically. Such people need to realize that God's justice against our sin has been satisfied by the suffering of Jesus Who suffered and bled in our place (Isaiah 53:4-6). Because He was punished in our place, we have no need or right to punish ourselves.

Conclusion

It had been a challenging, but exhilarating week during which I had labored hard to put the finishing touches on my studies on how the gospel enables us to overcome anger. I was excited about how clearly the Bible explains how anger comes from our selfish judgmental hearts and how grace transforms us from angry people to gracious people. It had also been an exhausting week. In addition to my research and writing I counseled, prepared my sermon for Sunday, and attended our church's family camp in the nearby mountains (does it sound like I am starting to make an excuse for what was about to happen?). As we came down from the mountains on Saturday afternoon, I was looking forward to a restful evening as we recovered from a very busy week and prepared for the Lord's Day. Then my wife's cell phone rang. One of her counselees was in a major crisis which required us to go see her family that afternoon.

As I was adjusting to this unforeseen change in my plans, I pulled onto our street hoping that our young adult son had kept things in good order in the house while we had been away. As we pulled into the driveway, I noticed our son's car was gone and a pile of newspapers sat on our yard announcing to all that our house was vacant and available to any thieves who wanted to visit. Then when we walked into the house, it looked like packs of angry raccoons had torn through every room leaving destruction in their wake. Alas, it was not raccoons, but it was our (absent) son. Dishes were piled high all over the kitchen and in the living room. Clothes and other debris littered the floor. Perishable food had been left open and out in various places. It couldn't have been thieves and vandals because nothing had been taken. To top it off, there was no note explaining our son's absence and he did not answer his mobile phone.

As a man who had just finished an extensive study on what the Bible says about sinful anger, I was very surprised at what suddenly went on in my own heart. I literally felt myself get hot. My pulse quickened. My mind raced as I began to compose a statement of judicial condemnation upon my son which would have equaled that of any Old Testament prophet decrying the sins of

Israel. After all of the benefits my son had received from us, how could he break covenant with us so egregiously? I also began to devise the sanctions I would bring upon him. I would cut off his cell phone, take away his car, kick him out of the house, and pile his every belonging on the front porch for him to get before Monday morning at which time Salvation Army would haul away the rest. The more I thought, the angrier I became.

Then I remembered what I had learned about overcoming anger with gospel grace, and started reciting the key things I need to tell myself when angry.

I wanted something too much (James 4:1-2), in this case it was a tidy house and a thoughtful son. While these are not evil desires, they became idolatrous when I was willing to sin because I did not get them.

I am not judge (Genesis 50:19 James 1:20). While some consequences would be appropriate for the mess we found, my desire to vent my anger by verbally condemning my son was not godly and would not be helpful.

God has shown great mercy to me (Ephesians 4:31-32; Matthew 18:21-35). Remembering that I am the chief of sinners who has been forgiven an infinite debt, I am called by God to deal with others in a way that reflects His mercy and grace to me.

God is in control and has a good plan (Romans 8:28; Genesis 50:20). God has allowed this bad thing to happen for His good purpose. His purpose in this trial is to strengthen my faith and to bring me to greater maturity in Christlikeness (James 1:2-4).

Remember who I am (Romans 6:11; 2 Corinthians 5:17). I am not the angry out-of- control man I used to be. My old self has died with Christ and I am a new man with a new nature, set free from sin's bondage. I can do all things through Christ Who strengthens me (Philippians 4:13).

By God's grace my heart was calmed. When our son finally got home I was able to listen to his explanation of why the house was a wreck (he was suddenly called in to work, and he didn't think we'd be home until evening). He sought our forgiveness and we worked together to straighten the house. And I gave thanks to God for how the gospel is changing me!

Personal Application Projects

1. What must you have or else you might sin because you don't get it (James 4:1-2)? Here are some examples...

» Be respected and appreciated

» Be happy and comfortable

» Be pain free

» Be successful

» Be safe

» Be treated fairly

» Be free from problems and pressures

» Be sexually fulfilled

» Be physically fit

» Not have others waste my time

» Have successful obedient children who make me look good

» Have a well-paying satisfying job

» Have a spouse who is affectionate

»   Have a tidy house

»   Have a spouse who is on time

»   Have plenty of money

»   Have the privacy I desire

»   Have a position of leadership in church

»   Have fun

»   Have what I want to eat

»   Not be cut off in traffic

2. Memorize Ephesians 4:31-32 to remind you of how the gospel makes you forgiving and gracious.

3. Make a list of five ways you can show love in your words and actions to those who have hurt or disappointed you.

4. Create a notecard (or a document on your mobile phone) with the five important truths you need to remember (with related Scriptures) when you are tempted to be angry. Keep this notecard with you and prayerfully read it when you feel the temptation to become angry.

5. *Keep an anger journal for each time your anger gets out of control.[21] Include the following questions:*

» What were the circumstances when I became angry?

» What did I say to my own heart? What did I want? James. 4:1-2

» What did I say/do when I felt provoked?

» What is a biblical evaluation of what I said and did?

» What should I have said to myself when I felt angry?

» What should I have said and done when I felt provoked?

» What do I need to do now to make things right?

Where Can I Get More Help?

BOOKS

Adams, Jay, *From Forgiven to Forgiving: Learning to Forgive One Another God's Way* (Amityville, NY: Calvary Press, 1994)

Brauns, Chris, *Unpacking Forgiveness: Biblical Answers for Complex Questions and Deep Wounds* (Wheaton, IL: Crossway, 2008)

MacArthur, John, *The Freedom and Power of Forgiveness* (Wheaton, IL: Crossway, 2009)

Sande, Ken, *The Peacemaker: A Biblical Guide to Resolving Personal Conflict* (Grand Rapids: Baker, 2004)

ARTICLES

Crater, Tim, "Counsel on Being Reconciled to Our Brother," in *Journal of Pastoral Practice*, 5/3 (1982), 25–34

Lane, Tim, "Pursuing and Granting Forgiveness," in *Journal of Biblical Counseling*, 23/2 (2005), 52–59

WEB SITES

Peacemaker Ministries: www.hispeace.org

Christian Counseling Education Foundation: www.ccef.org

Notes

1   Adams, Jay, *The Christian Counselor's Manual*,
    (Phillipsburg, NJ, Presbyterian and Reformed, 1973) p.
    359

2   American Psychological Association, *Controlling Anger
    before it Controls You*, http://www.apa.org/topics/
    anger/control.aspx

3   Jones, Robert D, *Uprooting Anger*, (Phillipsburg, NJ,
    Presbyterian and Reformed, 2005), p. 15.

4   American Psychological Association, *Controlling Anger
    before it Controls You*, http://www.apa.org/topics/
    anger/control.aspx

5   Ibid

6   Jones, Robert D, *Uprooting Anger*, (Phillipsburg, NJ,
    Presbyterian and Reformed, 2005), p.29-30 .

7   Spurgeon, CH, *Morning by Morning*, p. 207 (July 13)
    http://books.google.com/books

8   Ibid

9   In the same way a substance abuser or a sex offender
    may claim to have certain strong innate drives or past
    experiences which have made these sins harder to resist.

10 American Psychological Association, *Controlling Anger
    before it Controls You*, http://www.apa.org/topics/
    anger/control.aspx

11 Ibid

12 Ibid

13 Ibid

14 It seems very unlikely that Jacob would have told the brothers and not Joseph this, especially in light of the close relationship they shared and the time they spent together (Genesis 48).

15 A talent was more than fifteen years' wages. Given that the median income in the US is about $51,000 per year (as of 2011) ten thousand talents would be over $7.5 billion (thousand million). http://quickfacts.census.gov/qfd/states/00000.html

16 Given that a dinar was a day's wage, one hundred dinarri would be approximately one third of a year's wage, or about $17,000 in today's dollars (see above).

17 For a more thorough explanation, read, *Help! I Want to Change*, by Jim Newheiser (Shepherd Press, 2012).

18 Adams, Jay, *What Do You Do When Anger Gets the Upper Hand?*, (Phillipsburg, NJ, Presbyterian and Reformed, 1975).

19 Ibid.

20 A parallel might be that a man may be tempted to lust when he sees a beautiful but immodest woman. He can either choose to dwell upon a sinful fantasy, or he can speak truth to his own heart as he turns away from looking at or thinking of her and chooses to dwell on more profitable things (Philippians 4:8-9).

21 These questions are based upon Lou Priolo's Anger Journal in his book, *The Heart of Anger*, (Calvary Press, 1998).

For more biblical counseling resources go to www.ibcd.org.

BOOKS IN THE HELP! SERIES INCLUDE...

Help! He's Struggling with Pornography
ISBN 978-1-63342-003-8

Help! Someone I Love Has Been Abused
ISBN 978-1-63342-006-9

Help! My Toddler Rules the House
ISBN 978-1-63342-009-0

Help! Someone I Love Has Cancer
ISBN 978-1-63342-012-0

Help! I Want to Change
ISBN 978-1-63342-015-1

Help! My Spouse Has Been Unfaithful
ISBN 978-1-63342-018-2

Help! I Have Breast Cancer
ISBN 978-1-63342-024-3

Help! I'm a Slave to Food
978-1-63342-027-4

Help! My Teen Struggles With Same-Sex Attractions
ISBN 978-1-63342-030-4

Help! She's Struggling With Pornography
ISBN 978-1-63342-033-5

Help! I Can't Get Motivated
ISBN 978-1-63342-036-6

Help! I'm a Single Mom
ISBN 978-1-63342-039-7

Help! I'm Confused About Dating
ISBN 978-1-63342-042-7

Help! I'm Drowning in Debt
ISBN 978-1-63342-045-8

Help! My Teen is Rebellious
ISBN 978-1-63342-048-9

Help! I'm Depressed
ISBN 978-1-63342-051-9

Help! I'm Living With Terminal Illness
ISBN 978-1-63342-054-0

Help! I Feel Ashamed
ISBN 978-1-63342-057-1

Help! I Want to Understand Submission
ISBN 978-1-63342-060-1

Help! Someone I Love Has Alzheimers
ISBN 978-1-63342-063-2

Help! I Can't Handle All These Trials
ISBN 978-1-63342-066-3

Help! I Can't Forgive
ISBN 978-1-63342-069-4

Help! My Friend is Suicidal
ISBN 978-1-63342-075-5

Help! I'm in a Conflict
ISBN 978-1-63342-078-6

Help! I Need a Good Church
ISBN 978-1-63342-081-6

(More titles in preparation)